D1399116

Nick Huckleberry Beak's Magnificent

Magic Tricks

southwater

99-34960

This edition is published by Southwater

Distributed in the UK by
The Manning Partnership
251–253 London Road East
Batheaston
Bath BA1 7RL
tel. 01225 852 727
fax 01225 852 852

Published in the USA by
Anness Publishing Inc.
27 West 20th Street
Suite 504
New York
NY 10011
fax 212 807 6813

Distributed in Canada by
General Publishing
895 Don Mills Road
400–402 Park Centre
Toronto, Ontario M3C 1W3
tel. 416 445 3333
fax 416 445 5991

Distributed in Australia by
Sandstone Publishing
Unit 1, 360 Norton Street
Leichhardt
New South Wales 2040
tel. 02 9560 7888
fax 02 9560 7488

Southwater is an imprint of Anness Publishing Limited
Hermes House, 88–89 Blackfriars Road, London SE1 8HA
tel. 020 7401 2077; fax 020 7633 9499

© 1997, 2001 Anness Publishing Limited

Publisher: Joanna Lorenz
Editor: Lyn Coutts
Photographer: Tim Ridley
Designer: Michael R. Carter
Jacket Design: The Bridgewater Book Company Limited

Previously published as *Magic Fun*

3 5 7 9 10 8 6 4 2

Introduction

Just saying the word *magic* makes you feel that something wonderful is going to happen – and it will! How do I know this? Because I am a magician, and I am going to show you how to do some of the best and funniest magic tricks around.

It takes just three things to make a magic show – an audience, a pocketful of good tricks and YOU! A great magician does not need flashy wands, fluffy bunnies and expensive magic sets. All you need is enthusiasm and practice. Almost all of the tricks in this book can be done using odds and ends found in your own home.

I know you are going to have lots of fun entertaining your friends and family with these magic tricks. But be warned – once you start, your audience will keep on asking for more. Happy magic!

Nick Huckleberry Beak

Contents

Materials

Watch

CARDBOARD
You will need sheets of thin white and colored cardboard to complete the projects in this book. You can buy large sheets of cardboard at stationery stores or recycle cardboard from cereal boxes and other types of packaging.

ENVELOPES
You will need one small envelope, 4 inches by 8 inches and a large envelope about 8½ inches by 11 inches. The envelopes can be of any color.

MARKERS
A marker is a type of felt-tip pen that draws thick lines. If you do not have a marker, use an ordinary felt-tip pen instead.

PENCIL SHARPENER
All you need is the pencil sharpener that you take to school.

PAPER
You will need a few sheets of white, unlined paper to complete the projects in this book. You can substitute white drawing paper.

PAPER CLIPS
A good collection of paper clips is vital for any promising magician.

PENCIL
You will need an ordinary lead pencil for drawing and a rubber-tipped pencil to use in one of the tricks.

WHITE GLUE
This is a strong glue that can be used to stick together paper, wood or even fabric. It can bought at stationery stores and is sometimes called craft glue.

RECYCLED BOXES
For the projects in this book, you will need two empty boxes – one large and one small. A cereal box and a small tea box would be ideal. Ask for permission to use these boxes before you empty them.

RUBBER BANDS
To do the tricks in this book you will need large and small rubber bands. You can buy bags of assorted rubber bands at stationery stores.

Cardboard

White paper

Recycled boxes

RULER
A thin wood or plastic ruler is ideal.

SAFETY SCISSORS
Safety scissors are smaller than cutting scissors and they have colored plastic handles. Their edges are rounded and the blades are not as sharp as normal scissors.

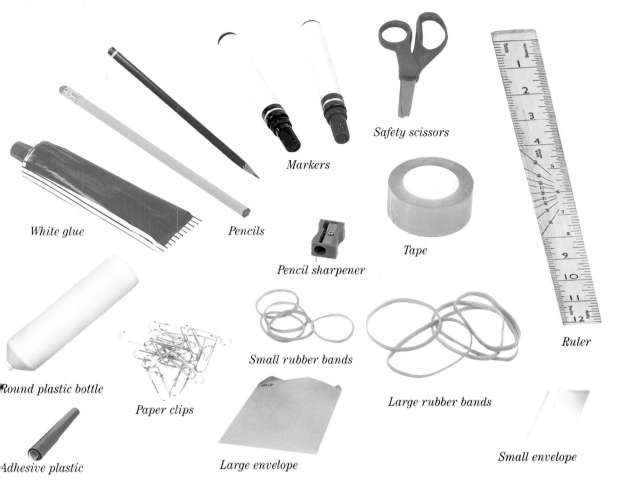

White glue

Pencils

Markers

Safety scissors

Pencil sharpener

Tape

Ruler

Round plastic bottle

Paper clips

Small rubber bands

Large rubber bands

Large envelope

Small envelope

Adhesive plastic

ADHESIVE PLASTIC

This material comes in many colors and designs. It is usually bought in rolls. To make it adhere to a surface, you simply peel off the protective backing paper and press the adhesive plastic onto the object. You can use leftover wrapping paper and white glue instead.

TAPE

You will need clear tape for the projects in this book.

CARDBOARD

You can get cardboard by recycling a cardboard box. Flatten the box and then ask an adult to cut along the folds. Cardboard can also be purchased at stationery stores.

ROUND PLASTIC BOTTLE

This plastic bottle needs to be straight-sided and about a foot tall. It must be wide enough so a ball can fall easily through it. A shampoo bottle is ideal.

WRISTWATCH

You will need a wristwatch or clock with a second hand.

Equipment

ARTIFICIAL ROSE
This rose is made from plastic or fabric. You can buy them at florists or garden centers.

FLEXIBLE STRAWS
Small accordian folds near one end of the straws allow them to bend. Once bent, they will stay in that position.

SMALL RUBBER BALL
This ball is sometimes called a superball. When it is dropped, it bounces very high.

CLEAR PLASTIC CUP
A disposable drinking cup is ideal, but it must be transparent.

CLIPBOARD
This is made from a piece of wood or thick plastic-covered cardboard. The paper is clamped to the clipboard by a metal clip.

COINS
You can use real or plastic toy money to do the magic tricks.

DETACHABLE PENCIL ERASER
This is a small eraser that slips onto the top of a pencil.

CHECKERS
These black and white round disks are made of wood or plastic and are used to play games such as checkers.

FINGER REEL
This is a special little device that makes objects fly back to their original position. Inside the finger reel is a fine thread that is attached to a spring-loaded reel. When you pull out the thread and then let it go, it will be pulled back inside the finger reel. Finger reels are very inexpensive. You can buy them at joke and toy stores.

GRAPES
It is best to use seedless grapes for the trick in this book. Always be careful when you put things in your mouth.

HANDKERCHIEFS
You can use large or small cotton handkerchiefs. Brightly colored or patterned ones are best for magic tricks.

HAT
You can use any sort of hat as long as it is tall and stiff.

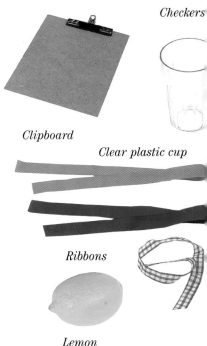

Clipboard

Clear plastic cup

Ribbons

Lemon

LEMON
You can use a real or plastic lemon to do the magic trick in this book.

LARGE PLAYING CARD
This is about four times the size of a normal playing card. You can buy them at joke and toy stores. To do all the tricks in this book, you will need two large playing cards.

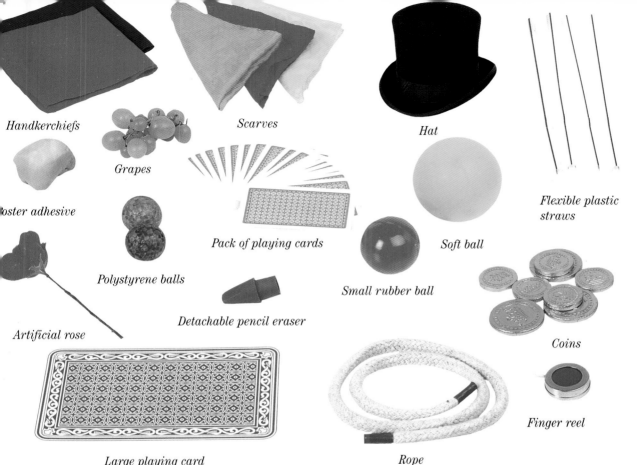

Handkerchiefs

Scarves

Hat

Grapes

Flexible plastic straws

oster adhesive

Pack of playing cards

Soft ball

Polystyrene balls

Small rubber ball

Detachable pencil eraser

Coins

Artificial rose

Large playing card

Rope

Finger reel

PACK OF PLAYING CARDS

A deck of playing cards consists of 52 cards plus two okers. There are four suits – hearts, diamonds, clubs and spades – numbered from ace o king. There are two black suits and two red suits. To do ll the tricks, you will need wo packs of cards. Playing ards are inexpensive and can be purchased at toy stores.

ROPE

You will need two pieces of white cotton rope. One should be 1 yard long, the other about 6 inches long. To prevent the ends from fraying, wind colored tape around them.

SCARVES

Soft, silky scarves in bright colors are ideal. You will need large and small scarves.

SOFT BALL

This ball is made from sponge or light plastic.

POSTER ADHESIVE

This reusable material is used to stick posters onto walls.

POLYSTYRENE BALLS

These small, lightweight balls can be bought at craft stores.

Putting on a Show

To put on a really good magic show, you need to know the three Ps. No, not three garden peas, but the three magic Ps – preparation, presentation and performance. You can forget all about that abracadabra mumbo-jumbo. Just remember the three Ps.

PREPARATION

To avoid getting halfway through a really good trick and realizing that you are missing a vital piece of equipment, you must be prepared. You must have everything you will need at your fingertips. The only way that you can be properly prepared is to make a list of the items that are required for each trick. As you gather them, cross them off the list. Simple idea, but it works. Have you made your list yet? No? Then get to it!

PRESENTATION

This is about how you dress and act in front of your audience. Presentation is very important if you want your magic show to be a great success. To find out more about presentation, see pages 12–13.

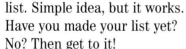

PERFORMANCE

You have decided to put on a show. Congratulations! The first thing you must do is decide on your tricks and the order you will do them in. There are no rules for this, but remember that a short show full of knock-out tricks is better than a long show with only a few good tricks.

The best and easiest way to give your magic show atmosphere is to use music. Try to match the speed and mood of the music to the pace

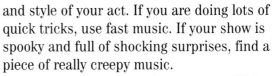

and style of your act. If you are doing lots of quick tricks, use fast music. If your show is spooky and full of shocking surprises, find a piece of really creepy music.

If you do not use music, then you will have to write a script and rehearse the words you are going to say. You may want to introduce each magic trick or tell a little story about where you learned a certain trick. But whatever you say, it is a good idea to have prepared it. It also never hurts to have a couple of jokes up your sleeve. These can be used to entertain your audience while you prepare your next trick. Do not use any bad jokes – only I am allowed to use those.

Magical Style

Even if you can do some of the hardest magic tricks in the world, your show might flop if your presentation style is boring. To be a big hit with an audience you have to have pizzazz and style. Problem is, you cannot buy pizzazz and style at a supermarket. I tried once and came out with two frozen pizzas instead. But presentation style is something you can learn.

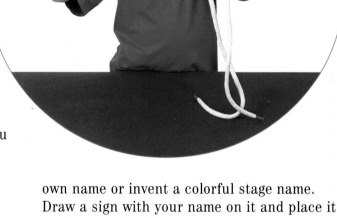

DRESS STYLE

The traditional costume for a magician is a stylish suit, bow tie and flashy cape. Nowadays, almost any sort of costume is fine. A colorful jacket and a pair of jeans can look just as hip and professional. If you want to wear your own wacky costume, go ahead. My rule is – if you feel good, you will look good.

STAGE STYLE

To be a show-stopping performer, you must know the secrets of the trade.

The first is, always enter from the side or back of the stage. Walk to the middle, smile at your audience and wait for the applause. I promise from the bottom of my wallet that your audience will clap.

The second thing to do is introduce yourself to the audience. You can use your own name or invent a colorful stage name. Draw a sign with your name on it and place it on the stage beside you.

Number three: Always face your audience. This will mean that your props, or equipment, will have to be within easy reach. Your audience has not come to watch you rummage around in a box.

The fourth trade secret is this – if you make a mistake or a trick does not work, run

or your life. I am only joking, of course. If
something goes wrong, try to laugh it off. You
can even pretend that the mistake was
meant to happen. Then you can do the
trick again, but this time do it
correctly. If you do not know what
went wrong, go on to the next trick.
After the show practice the trick
until you get it right.

The last tip is to let the
audience know you have finished a
trick by taking a small bow. Save
the big bow until the end. As soon
as they see you bow, the audience
will clap and call out for more. Smile
and thank your audience for being so
much fun.

ENTERTAINING STYLE

This one is easy to explain. If you have
a smile on your face and look as though
you are enjoying what you are doing,
the audience will also enjoy
themselves. Try to look confident
and relaxed. When you
talk to your audience,
speak clearly and
loudly. No one will hear
your great jokes if you
mumble and mutter.

PROFESSIONAL STYLE

If the audience asks you to repeat
a trick, refuse politely. (A trick is
never as good the second-time
around.) Instead, move on to your
next trick and tell the audience
that this one is even better!

Magicians are always asked to
show how a trick works. Never
be tempted to give away the
secrets of your magical craft. If
you tell your secrets, you will
have to learn a whole
new routine.

13

Topsy-turvy Pencil

Are you ready to do your first magic trick? Great. It is really easy and will totally bamboozle your audience. The knack is to do the trick quickly so your audience does not have time to figure out how you did it. Sometimes magicians just have to be sneaky. The Topsy-turvy Pencil trick should be performed only once.

YOU WILL NEED
pencil
pencil sharpener
detachable pencil eraser

① Use the pencil sharpener to sharpen the blunt end of the pencil. Make sure that both ends of the pencil look the same.

② Put the detachable pencil eraser onto one end of the pencil. Your pencil should look like an ordinary pencil. Only you and I know that it is not.

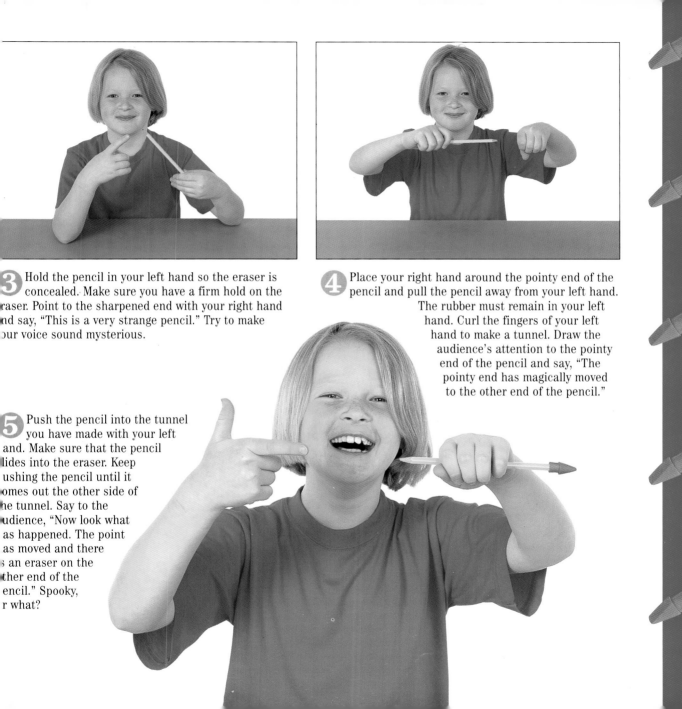

3 Hold the pencil in your left hand so the eraser is concealed. Make sure you have a firm hold on the eraser. Point to the sharpened end with your right hand and say, "This is a very strange pencil." Try to make your voice sound mysterious.

4 Place your right hand around the pointy end of the pencil and pull the pencil away from your left hand. The rubber must remain in your left hand. Curl the fingers of your left hand to make a tunnel. Draw the audience's attention to the pointy end of the pencil and say, "The pointy end has magically moved to the other end of the pencil."

5 Push the pencil into the tunnel you have made with your left hand. Make sure that the pencil slides into the eraser. Keep pushing the pencil until it comes out the other side of the tunnel. Say to the audience, "Now look what has happened. The point has moved and there is an eraser on the other end of the pencil." Spooky, or what?

Runaway Ribbon

I bet you are wondering what makes this piece of ribbon so special. Just you wait and see. I am sure this trick will impress you as much as your audience. This is an excellent opening trick for a magic show. It is easy to do, and you can invite a member of the audience to assist you on stage.

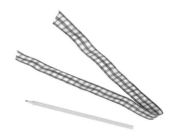

YOU WILL NEED
ribbon
pencil

1 Hold the pencil so the audience can see it clearly. Hang the ribbon over the pencil. Make sure that the length of ribbon nearest to you is longer. In a moment you will see why this is important.

2 Place one finger gently on the edge of ribbon where it lies over the pencil. Start turning the pencil so the ribbon winds around the pencil. You have to turn the pencil toward yourself.

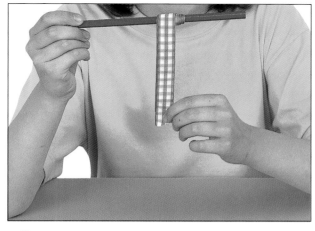

3 When most of the ribbon has been wound onto the pencil, the shorter section of ribbon will suddenly fall over the top of the pencil. As soon as this happens, stop turning the pencil. It is important that you practice this part of the trick to get your timing perfect.

4 A length of ribbon should now be hanging from the pencil, as shown. The rest of the ribbon will look as though it is wound around the pencil. Hold the pencil with one hand and the two ends of the ribbon with the other. Now get ready to impress your audience.

5 Pull the ribbon slowly to add to the suspense. Continue pulling until there is no ribbon on the pencil. Oh, wow! The ribbon has melted right through the pencil. Make sure that the audience can see that the ribbon has not been cut. Your reputation as a great magician will now spread far and wide.

HANDY HINT
You can invite a friend from the audience to assist you with this trick. It will be his or her job to hold the pencil while you pull the ribbon.

Hanky Pranky

This is one of my favorite magic tricks. To make the pencil look as though it is going through the handkerchief, all you need to do is create a secret gap between the handkerchief and your hand. Practice your sleight of hand in front of a mirror until it is so slick that you almost fool yourself.

YOU WILL NEED
handkerchief
pencil

1 Curl the fingers of your left hand to make a tunnel. Position your hand so the tunnel runs up and down. Lay the handkerchief over it. This is not the time to blow your nose. You need a clean hanky for this trick.

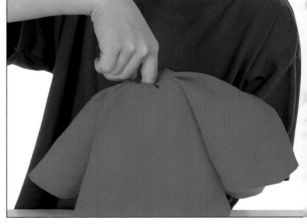

2 Push a little bit of the handkerchief into the tunnel. Do this using the fourth finger on your right hand. You should have made a small dip in the middle of the handkerchief. Do not move your finger just yet.

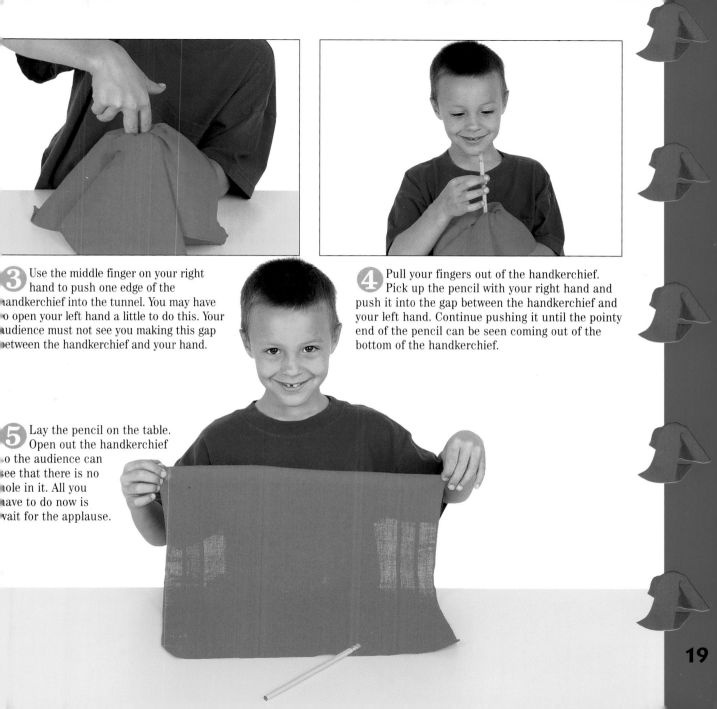

3 Use the middle finger on your right hand to push one edge of the handkerchief into the tunnel. You may have to open your left hand a little to do this. Your audience must not see you making this gap between the handkerchief and your hand.

4 Pull your fingers out of the handkerchief. Pick up the pencil with your right hand and push it into the gap between the handkerchief and your left hand. Continue pushing it until the pointy end of the pencil can be seen coming out of the bottom of the handkerchief.

5 Lay the pencil on the table. Open out the handkerchief so the audience can see that there is no hole in it. All you have to do now is wait for the applause.

Magic Knot

Here is your first trick using a piece of rope. There is a knack to pulling the scarf off the rope for the big finale, so you will need to practice this trick quite a few times before you perform it in front of friends and family. This trick is easier to do if you use a small, silky scarf.

YOU WILL NEED
1-yard length of rope
small soft scarf or handkerchief

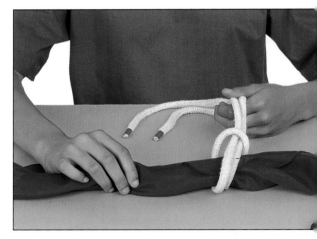

1 Fold the rope in half. Place your right hand about halfway along the rope to keep the rope still. Pick up the loop in your left hand and fold it over your right hand. Keep your right hand in the same position. Place the loop over the ends and thread the ends through the loop. Pull gently to close the loop a little. The rope must not be twisted or crossed.

2 Leave the rope with its loop on the table. Fold the scarf or large handkerchief diagonally in half. Continue folding until the scarf is narrow enough to fit easily through the loop. Thread the scarf through the loop. Gently pull on the ends of the rope to close the loop around the center of the scarf – do not pull it very tight. Try not to twist the rope.

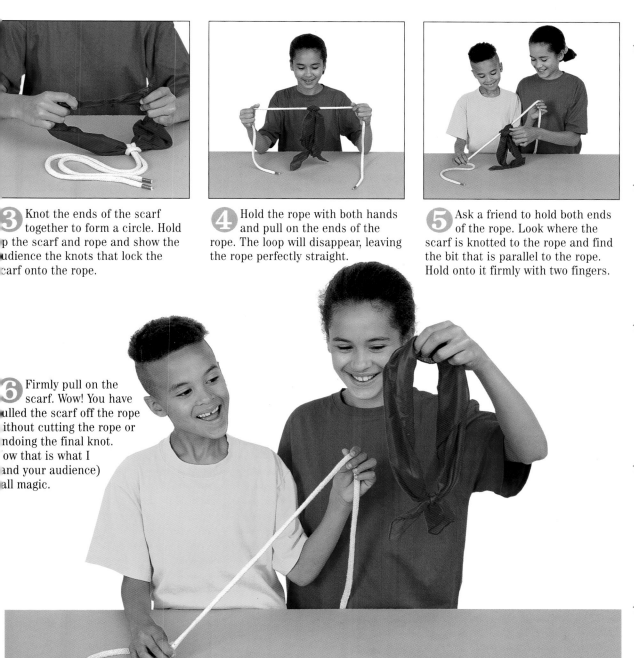

3 Knot the ends of the scarf together to form a circle. Hold up the scarf and rope and show the audience the knots that lock the scarf onto the rope.

4 Hold the rope with both hands and pull on the ends of the rope. The loop will disappear, leaving the rope perfectly straight.

5 Ask a friend to hold both ends of the rope. Look where the scarf is knotted to the rope and find the bit that is parallel to the rope. Hold onto it firmly with two fingers.

6 Firmly pull on the scarf. Wow! You have pulled the scarf off the rope without cutting the rope or undoing the final knot. Now that is what I (and your audience) call magic.

Slippery Knot

This trick will take lots of practice. You have to be able to make the false knot without a hitch. Read the instructions carefully so you know exactly how to hold the rope. To make sure your audience never catches a glimpse of the knotted rope in your right hand, try to keep the back of your right hand facing the audience.

YOU WILL NEED

1-yard length of rope
6 inches of identical rope with a knot in the middle

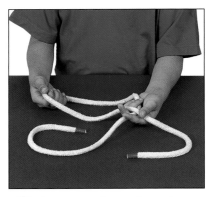

1 Conceal the knotted rope in your right hand. Lay the other rope on the table and make a loop. Hold the rope in your left hand, as shown. The thumb should be firmly placed over where the rope crosses itself. The first and second fingers should be inside the loop. The end of the lower section of rope should pass between the third and fourth fingers.

2 Use your right hand to thread the end of the lower rope into the loop. It must pass under the rope that forms the loop, as shown. Move the second finger so it squeezes the upper rope against the third finger. Keep a firm pressure on the rope with the fingers of the left hand while the rope is being pulled by the right hand.

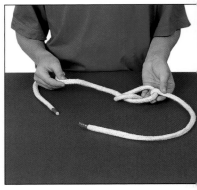

3 Before the knot becomes too tight, slide your second finger under the rope that is being pulled. This will take lots of practice. Keep holding the rope between the thumb and fourth finger. The first and third fingers can be moved out of the way. Keep pulling on the rope so it closes around the second finger. Carefully pull out your second finger.

4 Keep holding the rope between thumb and fourth finger. The knotted rope in your right hand must remain hidden from the audience.

5 Close your right hand around the long piece of rope just above the knot. Slide this hand down the rope. As your hand passes over the false knot, the knot will disappear. Slide your hand all the way to the bottom of the rope.

6 When your right hand reaches the bottom of the rope, pretend to pull the knot off the rope. Throw the knot that you have been hiding in your hand all along to your audience. They will be impressed, I promise.

HANDY HINT

To make it easy to conceal the knotted rope, tie the knot as small as possible. Then trim any excess rope from either side of the knot.

23

Wacky Knots

The first part of this trick is how to tie a knot in a length of rope without letting go of the ends. The second part shows you how to tie a knot using only one hand. When you have mastered them, challenge your friends to copy your feats of dexterity. It is bound to cause some chuckles as your friends tie themselves up in nutty knots.

YOU WILL NEED
1-yard length of rope

1 **Wacky knot number 1** – Lay the rope on the table and fold your arms, as shown. One hand should be tucked under one arm, the other hand should be resting on top of the other arm.

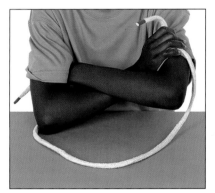

2 Without uncrossing your arms, pick up one end of the rope with each hand. You will have to lean over the table so your hands are within reach of the ends of the rope.

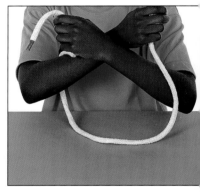

3 When you have twisted and squirmed enough to pick up the ends of the rope, start to uncross your arms. Do not do this too fast, or the rope will snag and you will have to start again.

4 When your arms are uncrossed, you will see that you have made a knot in the rope. What? No knot? Then you did not cross your arms correctly. Give it another try.

5 **Wacky knot number 2** – To make a knot using only one hand, hold the rope as shown. I have been doing this trick for ages, which is why I am called Nicky Tricky Fingers.

6 Tightly curl your third and fourth fingers over the rope. Make sure they are holding the rope firmly. Open your first and second fingers like a pair of scissors.

7 Flick your wrist so the end of the rope nearest you falls over the back of your hand. Reach down with your scissor fingers and take hold of this shorter length of rope. Let go of the rope you are holding with your third and fourth fingers.

8 Lower your hand so your fingers point down. Jiggle your hand so the rope over the back of your hand falls forward. As the rope passes the short end of rope held between your scissor fingers, it will make a knot.

Missing Money

This trick is every magician's favorite. Why? Because it cannot go wrong. All you need are five coins and some tape stuck to the palm of your hand. Remember to keep the palm of your hand concealed throughout the trick, otherwise the audience will figure out your secret.

YOU WILL NEED
5 small coins of the same size
strong, clear tape

1 Cut a small piece of tape. Overlap the ends, sticky side out, to make a loop. Place the five coins in front of you on the table.

2 Firmly press the loop of tape onto the palm of your hand. Do not let anyone see you doing this. This little bit of sneakiness is just between you and me.

3 Make a big show of counting the five coins one-by-one as you stack them one on top of another. Ask the audience to count along with you.

4 Press the hand with the sticky loop onto the pile of coins. Say your chosen magic words and then withdraw your hand. The top coin will be stuck to the loop.

5 Keep the palm concealing the coin flat on the table. Slowly spread out the pile of coins and count them out loud. Yikes! There are now only four coins.

6 You, of course, know exactly where the fifth coin has gone. It is hiding in the palm of your hand. Remove this coin when you return the other coins to your pocket or to your magic box.

HANDY HINT

In place of a loop of tape, you can use a small piece of double-sided tape. Use small coins rather than large ones. You can use plastic coins if you want to.

Where is the Coin?

This is a trick you see magicians perform on stage or on television. It involves sleight of hand and more than a little bit of sneakiness. You must convince the audience that the coin is in the cup by making sure they hear it fall into the cup. But is the coin in the cup? No way!

YOU WILL NEED
large scarf or handkerchief
coin
clear plastic cup

1 Hold your right hand with your fingers pointing upward. Place the middle of the scarf or handkerchief over your hand. Position the coin on the scarf so you can grip it with the fingers of your right hand.

2 Hold the cup in your left hand. Place the scarf upside down over the cup so the scarf hides the cup. Let go of the coin. It will make a sound as though it has fallen into the cup. What has really happened is this ...

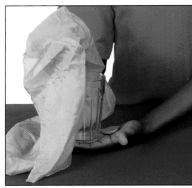

3 When you cover the cup with the scarf, tilt the cup away from you. When you let go of the coin, it does not fall into the cup but drops onto the side of the cup, makes a noise and then falls into your left hand. Double sneaky!

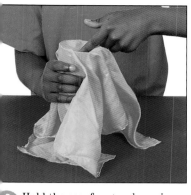

4 Hold the scarf-covered cup in your right hand. Use the refinger of your left hand (do not rget that the coin is concealed in is hand) to make a dip in the middle the scarf. You can invite someone om the audience to do this.

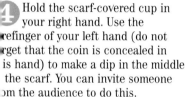

5 Look at the cup and say, "This dip should be just a little deeper." Then push your left hand farther down into the cup and release the coin. Make sure the coin does not bump against the cup and make a noise.

6 Bring your left hand out of the cup and ntly pull the front of the arf downward. As you , the coin will come to e top of the cup. You n also pull the scarf ickly so that the coin erally jumps out of the p. Whichever way you do this trick is always a al treat.

HANDY HINT

When you conceal a coin in your hand, it is called palming. To palm the coin swiftly and secretly takes skill. Practice in front of a mirror until you can fool yourself.

29

Handful of Coins

Handful of Coins may seem easy, but it takes time and effort to make every gesture totally convincing. This is another magic trick that you should practice in front of a mirror. When you think you have mastered it, perform it for a friend before including it in your magic show.

YOU WILL NEED
a large pile of coins

1 Place the pile of coins on the table in front of you. Lay your hands palm down on the table.

2 Pretend to pick up a coin with your right hand. Your movements must be convincing.

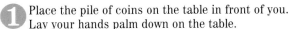

3 Place the nonexistent coin in the center of your left hand. Look carefully at the picture above to see how you should position your fingers and hands.

4 Form a fist with your left hand. Point to your left fist with the forefinger of your right hand. Tell the audience that you are going to make the coin disappear.

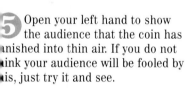

5 Open your left hand to show the audience that the coin has vanished into thin air. If you do not think your audience will be fooled by this, just try it and see.

31

Quick Separation

This game will really test your hand and eye coordination. The aim is to separate a stack of checkers into two piles in the shortest possible time. After you have practiced doing this, challenge your classmates to a friendly game of Quick Separation. You will need to ask someone to be timekeeper. Good luck!

YOU WILL NEED
4 black checkers
4 white checkers
ruler
watch or clock with a second hand

1 Stack the checkers one on top of the other, alternating black and white. Challenge your friends to separate the stack into a black pile and a white pile in the shortest possible time. No matter how quick they are, you will be quicker.

2 This is how you will do it. Hold the ruler flat on the table and slide it under the stack of checkers. Then quickly flick the ruler from side to side. The black pieces will go to one side and the white pieces to the other side.

3 The pieces will fly everywhere if your technique is not right. If you flick the ruler too slowly, the stack will topple over. If you flick the ruler too much, two or three pieces will fly off at the same time. There is only one way to get it right – to practice.

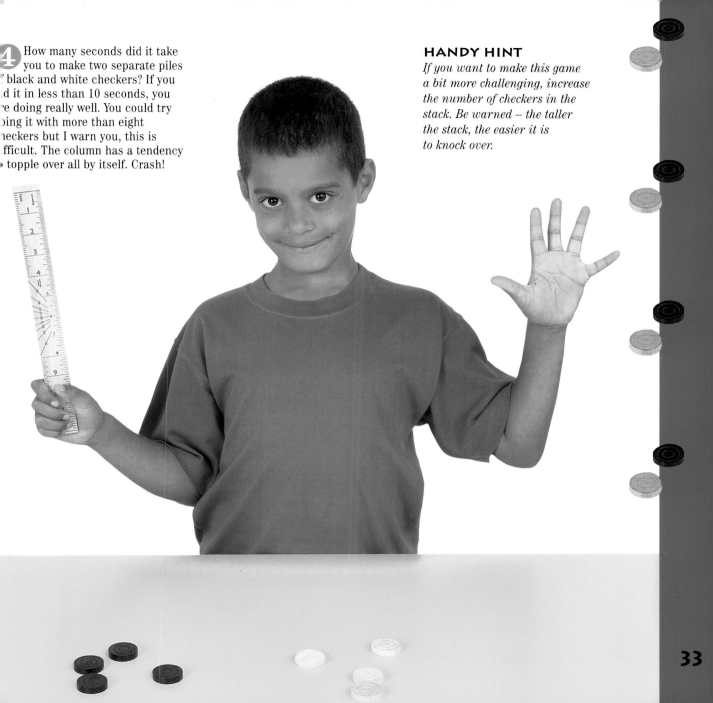

4 How many seconds did it take you to make two separate piles [of] black and white checkers? If you [di]d it in less than 10 seconds, you [ar]e doing really well. You could try [do]ing it with more than eight [ch]eckers but I warn you, this is [di]fficult. The column has a tendency [to] topple over all by itself. Crash!

HANDY HINT

If you want to make this game a bit more challenging, increase the number of checkers in the stack. Be warned – the taller the stack, the easier it is to knock over.

Keep It Under Your Hat

This is one of my silliest tricks. I make all my friends groan when I say I am going to do it. There is no need to practice this trick, but it is important to make a big show of muttering magical words and waving your hands over the hat. If you think you are an actor, this is your chance to prove it.

YOU WILL NEED

hat
clear plastic cup containing a drink

1 Ask a friend if they would like to watch you try out a fantastic new magic trick using a hat and a cup containing a drink.

2 Carefully place the hat over the cup. Tell your friend that you are going to drink the contents of the cup without touching the hat.

3 Say some magical words and wave your hands over the hat. Then announce that you have done the trick. Your friend will not believe you.

4 Your friend will most probably lift up the hat to see what has happened. If they do not, invite your friend to have a look under the hat.

5 As your friend lifts up the hat, quickly grab the cup and enjoy the drink. See, you did not have to touch the hat to get to the cup.

Hovering Ball

This is not so much a trick as a challenge. What you have to do is get a small ball to hover in the air above the end of a straw. Sounds easy, but it actually takes a lot of patience to get the stream of air just right if it is to hold the ball up. If you are willing to huff and puff in the name of scientific discovery, this challenge is for you!

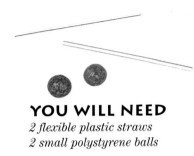

YOU WILL NEED
2 flexible plastic straws
2 small polystyrene balls

1 Bend the straw to form a right angle. I can guarantee that your friends and family will not know what is going to happen next.

2 Place the straw in your mouth and hold the ball jus over the end. Get ready to blow a steady stream of air down the straw.

3 Let go of the ball and see how long you can keep
  it hovering in the stream of air coming out of
the end of the straw. If you blow too hard, the ball
will shoot up quickly and then fall to the ground.
The ball will hover for longer if the stream of air
is soft but even.

4 So you think you are pretty good at
  this, do you? Well, it must be time
to make it extra hard by using two straws
and two balls. Use the same technique as
before, but you will require a bit more huff and puff.
If "Daredevil" is your middle name, then why not try
three straws and three balls?

The Big Card Trick

You may have seen this trick performed many times, but now you will be able to do it yourself. You can choose any number or suit you want for the large playing card, but a card of the same number and suit must be at the top of your deck of playing cards. The two cards attached to the large card must be numerically smaller than the big card.

YOU WILL NEED

deck of playing cards
poster adhesive
large playing card
large envelope

1 To prepare for this trick, use a small piece of poster adhesive to attach a two and a four of any suit onto the back of the large ten of clubs card. Place them in the envelope. Also make sure that the ten of clubs is the top card on your deck of cards. Now let the show begin.

2 Invite someone from the audience to join you on stage and cut the deck of cards. No, not with a pair of scissors. To cut the cards, all your guest has to do is take a pile of cards off the top of the pack and lay them beside the remaining cards.

3 Place the bottom half of the deck on top of the other cards. Place it so that it is at right angles to the cut cards. This will show you where the deck was cut and where you will find the ten of clubs. Tell your guest that he or she will shortly see their secret card.

4 Remove the top cards from the pile and turn over the next card. Without looking at the card, show it to your guest. Tell them that they must remember what their secret card is.

5 Ask your guest to shuffle the cards as much as they like. When they are shuffled, you can put them into the envelope. This envelope contains the large card plus the two other smaller cards.

6 Tell your guest that you are going to find his or her secret card. Pull from the envelope the two card. Ask if this is the secret card. He or she will say no. You then ask, "Is it bigger than this?"

7 Put your hand into the envelope again, but this time pull out the four card. Repeat the routine as in step 6. It is now your big moment to astound and amuse everyone. Put your hand into the envelope again and pull out the large ten of clubs card. Show it to your guest and say, "Is this big enough?" You have shown your guest that you knew that their chosen card was the ten of clubs all the time.

HANDY HINT

You can make your own large playing card with stiff white cardboard and a black felt-tip marker. It does not matter what card you choose to draw, as long as it is the same as the top card on your deck of cards.

Predict-a-Card

This is one the cleverest card tricks I know. Your friends will not be able to figure out why the chosen card is always the red ace. They may try to outwit you, but they will never succeed because you have this game in the bag. To make this trick work, you have to arrange the cards in a special order and learn the secret method of counting.

YOU WILL NEED
5 black playing cards of either suit, numbered 2, 3, 4, 5 and 6
1 red ace playing card of either suit

1 To prepare for this trick you have to arrange the six cards in a particular order. The top two cards must be black and the third must be the red ace. The bottom three cards are all black. To lay out the cards, deal the cards working from left to right. This will mean that the red ace will be the third card from the left.

2 Now it is show time! Lay out the cards as explained in step 1. Do not forget to start on the left. The cards must be face down. Ask someone in the audience to think of their favorite number between one and six. It does not matter what number they choose because you are a magician.

3 The aim of this trick is to show that whatever number your friend chooses, the card will always be the red ace. If your friend chose the number three, count three cards from the left. Push that card forward.

4 Turn over the other five cards to show that they are all black. Turn over the chosen card to reveal that it is the only red card. Wow! Do not repeat the trick, just leave the audience guessing.

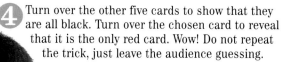

5 To make this trick work with any number your audience chooses, you have to remember these sneaky counting tricks. If your guest selects one, two or six, spell the number (o-n-e, t-w-o, s-i-x) instead of counting. For number one, the first card on the left would be 'o', the second would be 'n' and the third would be 'e.' If four is selected, count four cards starting from the right. If your guest picks five, spell five (f-i-v-e) starting with the first card on the right. No matter what the chosen number, you will always end up on the red ace.

Card Cascade

This is one of those tricks that will make your audience groan. As soon as they see all the cards unfold, they will know they have been conned. Sometimes magicians just have to be super crafty! To make the Card Cascade, use an old but complete deck of playing cards. Once the cascade is made, the cards cannot be used for anything else.

YOU WILL NEED
deck of playing cards
tape
large playing card
white glue

1 Divide the deck of playing cards into the four suits. Remove the jacks, queens, kings and jokers. Choose one suit and arrange the cards in numerical order from ace (one) to ten. Tape the cards end-to-end, as shown.

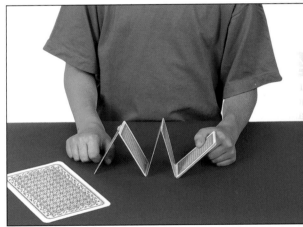

2 Fold up, accordian-style, the long line of taped cards. The cards should form a neat, flat pile. If they do not, carefully retape any cards that are overlapping or crooked.

3 Glue the back of the ace along the right hand edge of the large playing card. Repeat steps 2 and 3 for the remaining three suits of playing cards. When gluing the playing cards to the large card, alternate the colors and overlap the edges. If you take care when making the Card Cascade, you will have a trick that can be used again and again.

4 Hold up the large card with its back facing the audience. Keep a firm grip on the folded cards. You do not want them cascading down at the wrong moment. Ask someone to name a card of any suit between ace (one) and ten. Tell the audience that you are holding that very card in your hand right now. Turn the large card around and let the cards unfold. Point to the chosen card.

43

Magic Box

The Magic Box can produce objects out of thin air. One minute the box is empty, the next it is not. Only you know about the secret box that can hold a lemon, a pack of cards or even an elephant. If you are going to pull an elephant out of the box, perhaps this trick should be called the Magic Trunk!

YOU WILL NEED

1 small recycled box
1 large recycled box
tape
marker

ruler
scissors
white glue
adhesive plastic
lemon

1 To make the Magic Box, tape the ends of the boxes closed. Cut the top off the small box. Draw a line along one long and two short edges of the large box.

2 Cut along these lines carefully to make a hinged lid. By the way, did I tell you to empty the boxes before you started this project? Oops. Oh, well!

3 Do the same to the other side of the large box, but this time the hinged lid is on the opposite edge. You must get this right or the Magic Box will not be very magical.

4 Tape, glue or nail the small box securely to the inside of ~~ne~~ of the hinged lids. (Forget ~~n~~ailing – I was just joking.) The ~~op~~ened top of the small box must ~~fa~~ce where the lid is hinged.

5 Cover the box with adhesive plastic. Cut two strips of adhesive plastic to make tabs. Attach them to the outside edge of the lids, fold the tabs in half and attach to the inside edge. Put the lemon in the small box.

6 Now you are ready to make magic! Place the box on the table. The lid containing the small box is on the bottom with the tab nearest you. Hold on to both tabs because you are about to open the box.

7 Raise the Magic Box as you pull on the tabs. Now show ~~yo~~ur ugly, I mean, beautiful face in ~~th~~e hole. Say to the audience, "See, ~~th~~is box is empty – but not for long."

8 Carefully put the box back onto the table with the lid containing the lemon on the bottom. Then turn the box around. (The tab nearest you will be on the top lid.) Hold onto that tab and lift the lid. Pull the lemon out with a great flourish and show it to the audience.

45

Tricky Tubes

This is another classic trick that is used by magicians everywhere. It involves moving a handkerchief from one tube to another tube to give the impression that both tubes are empty. In the finale of this trick you stun the audience by producing a handkerchief from the empty tubes. To make this magical miracle you need only cardboard, paper clips, a rubber band and a handkerchief.

YOU WILL NEED

2 pieces of different colored cardboard, 12 x 12 inches
9 paper clips
rubber band
small handkerchief

1 Steps 1, 2 and 3 show the preparation you will need to do for this trick. Roll the two pieces of cardboard to make tubes. One tube must be narrower so that it will fit inside the larger tube. Secure the tubes with eight paper clips.

2 The device that makes this trick work is an ordinary paper clip. Unfold the paper clip to make hooks at either end, as shown. Attach a rubber band to one hook. Roll up the handkerchief and thread it into the rubber band.

3 Hook the other end of the paper clip onto the top of the narrow tube. The rubber band and the handkerchief will be on the inside of the tube. Make sure the handkerchief is totally hidden from view.

4. Now it is time to get this show on the road! Hold up the large tube so the audience can see it is empty. This should not be difficult, as it really is empty!

5. Pick up the narrow tube and slide it down through the large tube. As you do this, the hook holding the handkerchief will hook onto the side of the large tube.

6. Pull the narrow tube out from the bottom of the large tube. Hold up the narrow tube to show your audience it is empty.

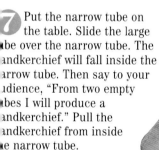

7. Put the narrow tube on the table. Slide the large tube over the narrow tube. The handkerchief will fall inside the narrow tube. Then say to your audience, "From two empty tubes I will produce a handkerchief." Pull the handkerchief from inside the narrow tube.

47

Half and Half

This is the only trick in this book that involves chopping something into pieces. What shall we use? Your sister or brother? No, they would be too messy. Let us start with something easy like a playing card and ribbon. The sneaky thing about this trick is that you never ever cut the ribbon.

YOU WILL NEED
a playing card
shiny, smooth ribbon
safety scissors

1 Fold the playing card in half lengthwise. Run your finger over the fold to flatten it.

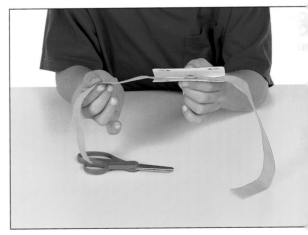

2 Lay the ribbon inside the folded card. The ends of the ribbon should hang from either side of the card.

3 Hold the card and ribbon in one hand. Pick up the safety scissors and cut across the center of the card and the ribbon. Always cut the folded edge first.

4 Your audience will not believe their eyes. The safety scissors have cut the card in two, but the ribbon remains in one piece. I do not know why this trick works, it just does!

49

Joke in the Mail

Want to send someone a shocking surprise? All it takes is paper, paper clips and tape. Joke in the Mail is so easy to assemble that you could make one for each of your friends. But will they still be your friends after you have played this joke on them? Always be careful when you are bending paper clips as the ends of the wire are sharp.

YOU WILL NEED
paper or thin cardboard
3 paperclips
tape
2 small rubber bands
1 small envelope
felt-tip marker

1 Fold the sheet of paper or thin cardboard into thirds. Press the folds flat and then open out the paper again.

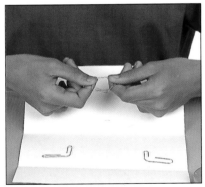

2 Open out two paper clips to make L-shapes, as shown. Bend and shape another paper clip to make a circle.

3 Tape the L-shaped paper clips to the paper and loop rubber bands around the ends, as shown. Thread the rubber bands onto the wire circle.

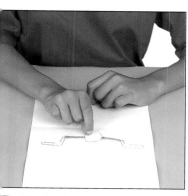

4 Slowly wind the wire circle around and around. The rubber [ba]nds will twist and tighten. Whatever [yo]u do, do not let go!

5 Fold the paper without letting go of the wire circle. Insert the folded paper into the envelope and seal it.

6 Address the envelope using the marker. Mail or deliver the envelope to your friend. Boy, is your friend in for a surprise!

7 When your friend opens [th]e letter, the rubber [ba]nds will unwind [ca]using the wire circle [to] make a loud noise as [it c]latters against the [pa]per. This is [bou]nd to give [you]r friend a [big] scare.

Gobble the Grape

Just when you thought things could not get any sillier, here is my all-time famous grape trick! To do this trick well you have to be able to pretend that you are holding a grape when, in fact, your hand is empty. This sounds easy, but it does require practice. I have been doing this trick for years and I still practice it before a show.

YOU WILL NEED
two small seedless grapes

1 Carefully place one of the grapes in your mouth. You must do this without your audience seeing. It is crucial that they think there is only one grape.

2 The show begins. Pick up the remaining grape in your right hand. Show the grape to the audience and then pretend to place it in your left hand.

52

3 Form a loose fist with your left hand to hide the grape that is not there. Point to your left hand with the forefinger of your right hand. Do not try to talk during this trick – the grape in your mouth will pop out!

4 Put your left hand on to your head and pretend to squash the grape. If you spread your fingers as you press down it makes it look as though you have really squashed the grape.

5 Open your mouth to reveal the grape. If you have carried off this joke convincingly the audience will think that the grape has moved through your head and into your mouth. Pretend to take the grape from your mouth with the right hand. Hold out your right hand and show the audience the grape that has been there since the beginning of the trick. You can now do the trick all over again.

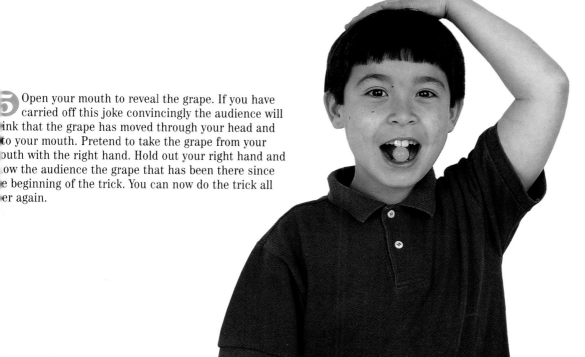

Mental Magic

In this trick you are going to read your friend's mind. You will not find out their deepest secrets, but you will discover your friend's chosen number. You must promise never to reveal the magical secret to anyone. If you break your promise, I will know, because I can read your mind.

YOU WILL NEED
sheet of paper
ruler
felt-tip marker
clipboard

HANDY HINT
You can do this trick in different ways. You can draw magic symbols around the numbers and then pretend to be deep in concentration. Or you can ask two or three friends to think of numbers at the same time.

1	2	4	8
7	6	13	10
5	3	15	14
3	15	7	13
11	7	6	15
9	10	5	12
13	14	12	11
15	11	14	9

1 Clamp the sheet of paper to the clipboard. With the ruler, draw three lines down it to make four columns. Copy the numbers in the picture opposite onto he paper. You must copy the numbers exactly. If you get hem wrong, you will not be reading anybody's anything!

2 Ask a friend to think of a number between 1 and 15. He or she must keep the number a secret. Then ask your friend if the secret number is in column one. Remember the answer your friend gives you. Do the same for columns two, three and four. Some numbers are repeated so your friend's number could be in more than one column.

3 Without even looking at the columns of numbers you will be able to guess your friend's number immediately. This is how you do it. Memorize the number at the top of each column (1, 2, 4 and 8). Then, when you know in which columns the secret number appears, you just add the numbers at the top of those columns together. For example, if your friend's number appears in the last three columns just add 2 and 4 and 8. Your friend's number is 14. Mental Magic is just so easy!

55

Bouncing Hanky

This quick trick will give your audience a laugh. It works because no one expects the handkerchief to go zooming into outer space. The Bouncing Hanky trick is even funnier if you can look as surprised as your audience. Before you do this trick make sure that all breakable objects are moved a safe distance away.

YOU WILL NEED
large handkerchief
bouncy rubber ball
rubber band

1 To prepare for this trick, open the handkerchief and place the ball in the center.

2 Wind the rubber band around the handkerchief, just above the ball, to hold the ball in place.

3 In the middle of a show take the prepared handkerchief out of your pocket and pretend to low your nose. Make funny noises to get a laugh.

4 Hold the handkerchief so the audience cannot see the ball. Take the handkerchief away from your nose and drop it onto the table or floor.

5 Wow! Look at that handkerchief go where no other handkerchief has gone before! Bouncing Hanky is a good trick to have up your sleeve (ha, ha!) to add humor to your show.

Returning Rose

To make this joke work, you have to find a fall guy. A fall guy is the person on whom the joke is played. I suggest you do this by offering your friend the rose as a gift for helping you with a trick. Not that your pal will thank you for playing this joke on them. You can buy the finger reel at joke and toy stores.

YOU WILL NEED
finger reel
artificial rose
scissors

① To do this trick, you need to wear a shirt with buttons and buttonholes. Thread the line from the finger reel through an open buttonhole. The finger reel should be on the inside of your shirt, out of sight of the audience.

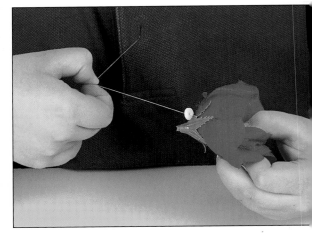

② Ask an adult to cut the stem off the artificial rose just below where the stem meets the flower. Securely tie the end of the finger reel line to the rose. If i is not tied tightly, the rose will fall off when the finger ree springs into action.

3 During the show ask a friend to assist you with a trick. To say thank you for their help, offer them the rose that is attached to your shirt or waistcoat. Gently pull the rose toward your friend's outstretched hand. Do not let go of the rose until it is in the palm of their hand.

4 Snap! Bang! Zoom! As soon as you release your hold on the rose, it will go zapping back to your shirt. Tee, hee, chuckle, chuckle!

Bottomless Tube

I do this trick when I am doing street performances because it is a good way to get people's attention. To make the Bottomless Tube, all you need is an empty plastic bottle. There is only one catch. The ball must be slightly smaller than the width of the bottle.

YOU WILL NEED
round plastic bottle (an empty shampoo bottle is ideal)
scissors
soft ball

1 To prepare for this trick, ask an adult to cut the top and bottom off the empty plastic bottle to make a tube. You can use a full container, but it is terribly messy and very wasteful. Decorate the tube if you want to.

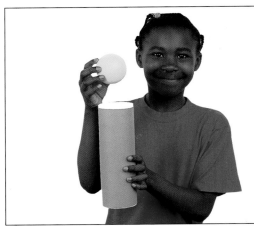

2 Let the show begin! Hold the tube up to the audience so they can see that it is empty. Then hold the tube and the ball, as shown. Get ready to drop the ball into the tube.

3 Drop the ball into the tube and quickly move your hand to the bottom of the tube so you can catch the ball as it comes out of the tube. You have to be quick, as the ball will not wait for you.

4 Repeat this routine until your audience begins to yawn. The next time you drop the ball into the tube, squeeze the tube gently so the ball cannot fall through the tube. Suddenly your audience will wake up. Where has the ball gone? Look perplexed as you peer into the tube. Then give the tube a shake. Just as you are about to give up the search for the ball, release your grip on the tube and let the ball fall out.

5 Sometimes I pretend not to notice that the ball is missing. I just keep repeating the dropping and catching routine until someone in the audience shouts, "The ball has vanished!" Then I release my grip on the tube and let the ball drop out. Okay, so maybe this is not very funny, but it keeps me happy.

Farewell Finale

Boo, hoo! It is time to go. The curtains are coming down on the greatest magic show on earth. So that you can say farewell to your audience in a magical way, I have prepared this special finale. It is important that you carefully follow the instructions for folding the paper. Fold it the wrong way and you will be saying goodbye to yourself.

YOU WILL NEED

2 sheets of paper
felt-tip marker
scissors
white glue

1 To prepare for this trick, place the sheet of paper with a long side nearest you. Draw a large picture of someone waving on the paper. Keep it simple because you will have to draw it again later on.

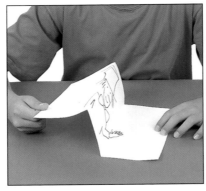

2 Turn the paper so the picture is upside-down. Fold the paper accordian-style, making the right hand flap a little larger than the other two. The right-hand flap is on the bottom, as shown.

3 Fold the paper away from you so the top flap is a little smaller than the bottom flap. I know this sounds really complicated, but i is actually easy. Do you think I coul do it if it was too hard? No way!

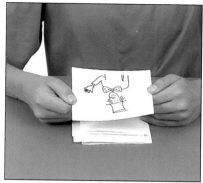

Take another sheet of paper and cut out a rectangle that is exactly the same size as the bottom flap of the folded paper. Onto this rectangle, draw the picture that is on the folded paper. See, I told you to keep it simple!

Glue this picture onto the front of the large flap. The bottom of the picture will be nearest the fold. Apply the glue carefully so it does not spread onto the other flaps. You are ready for your big finale!

Hold the paper, as shown, with the fold at the bottom and the small drawing facing the audience. To prevent the paper from unfolding, support the flap with a little finger. Tell the audience that you are going to give them a big farewell wave.

Quickly pull sideways so the folded paper unfolds and the large picture is revealed. Before their very eyes, the audience has seen the tiny farewell wave become a great, big farewell wave.

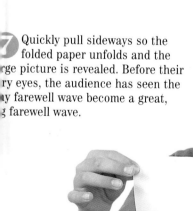

ACKNOWLEDGMENTS

The Publishers would like to thank the following children for modeling for this book:

Joshua Ashford
Lana Green
Reece Johnson
Alex Lindblom-Smith
Laura Masters
Laurence Ody
Yemisi Omolewa
Charlie Simpson
Frankie David Viner

Gratitude is also extended to their parents and the Walnut Tree Walk Primary School.

The author would like to thank Jonathon for being a brilliant magician and sharing his ideas; Christa, Nic, Kirsten, Paul and Francis for always being amazed by his tricks (Nick thinks that they are just being kind); and his brother, Mike – well, because someone has to!